J.R.Hamil

Farmland USA

Farmland USA

by James R. Hamil
and Harold Hamil

THE LOWELL PRESS / Kansas City, Missouri

Thanks to Many

Thanks to Many This book was made possible by the interest and encouragement of a list of people that could not possibly be identified by name. Some liked the idea from the first. Some asked critical questions that we considered seriously, and to our benefit, before going ahead. Many told us of scenes that might contribute to the beauty of this book.

One farmer pulled us out of the mud with his tractor. Another pumped some gasoline from his home tank for our car. A young man from a small town in Nebraska stopped his pickup and yanked us out of roadside sand. None would accept pay.

We were pleased and surprised by the enthusiasm of farm folk, industrialists, bankers and others to whom we explained what we were trying to do. We were gratified by the home-community pride we encountered. We were both surprised and pleased by the responses of men and women in remote places, men and women with a genuine appreciation of art as a part of rural America.

The country roads we've traveled—even when muddy—are lined with sentiment. Especially does that seem the case when we think of the friendly farmsteads where we have stopped. Country roads take people home in the full sense of the words of a popular song. And so we offer the picture on the following page as a sort of introduction to the rather strong nostalgic theme that runs through this book.

We thank all for their help and support.

— J.R.H., H.H.

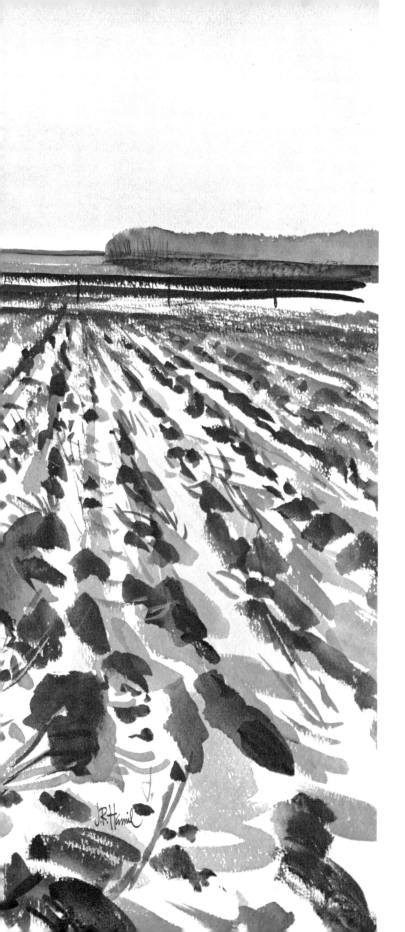

Contents

An Enchanting Circle in Mid-America

In Smith County, Kansas, near Lebanon and just a few miles south of the Nebraska border, is the generally recognized geographic center of the 48 states. From this spot, describe a circle on a 600-mile radius and you establish a rough boundary of the region covered by the paintings reproduced in this book.

This circle embraces an area of infinite variety. Its climate ranges from arid to semi-humid. Its terrain includes mountain peaks and low river bottoms. Its native flora ranges from sagebrush to towering oaks and pines. Its communities are made up of people from every ethnic strain the nation has known. But there is amazing unity here, based on a great common denominator: *agriculture*.

There is no other place in the world where a circle of 1,200 miles in diameter would enclose an area with agricultural production as advanced, as diverse and, at the same time, as well coordinated and articulated as it is here. There are highly productive regions in the U. S. outside this geographic middle, but the circle, we think, dramatizes and properly emphasizes the fact that our continental heartland and our agricultural heartland pretty well coincide.

Within this circle are all or parts of seven states which, year after year, rank among the first ten in annual value of agricultural production. A state within this circle (not always the same one) is consistently at the top in production of wheat, corn, cattle, hogs, soybeans, sorghum grains, cotton and rice. If there is a product common to all parts of the region, it could be cattle, or the grass, in infinite varieties, on which cattle feed.

This book, however, is not a book about commodities or their production. It is concerned primarily with what an artist sees as he criss-crosses this vast region. It is a book of glimpses, a book of impressions, a book of moods. It emphasizes the beauty of things prosaic, the charm of the commonplace, the grandeur of the plains and prairies and the nostalgia stirred by the decaying remains of some of man's additions to the landscape.

Besides the farmsteads, the fields and pastures, the feedlots, the market towns and larger cities of this agricultural heartland, there are rivers and lakes, to which an artist is naturally drawn.

The dominant geographic element of the region is probably the wide Missouri, winding many hundreds of miles and picking up the waters of the Chariton, the Osage, the Grand, the Kansas, the Platte, the Nishnabotna, the Big and Little Sioux, the Niobrara, the James and other streams, each draining a sizable watershed of its own.

On the western edge of our circle are high mountain valleys, some draining into the Platte, the Arkansas, and the Rio Grande and some, beyond the Continental Divide, into the Colorado. To the south and east are headwaters of the Cimarron, the two Canadians and other tributaries of the Arkansas, and farther around the arc are vast lands drained by the Red, the Trinity, the Brazos, the Pecos, and Texas' own Colorado. Cutting across our circle on the east, of course, is the Mississippi, largest of all.

These rivers relate to history and settlement. Lewis and Clark followed the Missouri to its origin and provided facts justifying President Jefferson's purchase of Louisiana Territory. Trappers, traders, military expeditions, homeseekers followed the rivers in turn. Some left the Missouri at the mouth of the Kansas and went on by wagon to Santa Fe or Oregon. Some set out from Omaha and St. Joseph, and from the latter for a brief period the Pony Express riders went westward to follow the Little Blue, the Platte and, beyond it, various mountain and desert trails to the Pacific.

Coronado traveled in this land, as did John C. Fremont, Zebulon Pike, Jim Bridger and Kit Carson.

Continued

New Corn Weathered hills in springtime green . . .black soil with new corn breaking through . . .and the well and windmill spotted in the lowest part of the field. The combination does not belong exclusively to western Iowa, but it's familiar there.

The largest buffalo herds roamed here, and the biggest slaughter of these noble animals took place here. Some of the sorriest chapters of our nation's relations with Indians were written within this circle. No less a person than Abraham Lincoln (as a captain of Illinois militia) was a participant in one of the earliest of a long series of campaigns that pushed the Indians westward from the Mississippi. Later, on a political mission, Mr. Lincoln visited eastern Kansas on what was considered a tour of the frontiers of civilization.

This region includes the first homestead taken under the law Mr. Lincoln signed in 1862. It includes tens of millions of acres settled under this federal program and many millions more made available during the systematic sale of land acquired by railroads as their reward from the government for pushing their lines across the monotonous, unsettled prairies.

The region is again in transition. Production methods have changed radically in recent years, and they continue to change. The countryside is changing. To some extent, it is giving up the picturesqueness for which it once was known. The big barns are not often restored when they fall into disrepair. Their replacements are more functional than decorative. The same can be said for some early-day fences. The old concrete-block silo gives way to underground storage or bright-colored steel tanks. But there was still much of the old to be captured in this book and preserved for posterity,

along with some of the new and modern scenes and silhouettes that mark rural Mid-America as it enters the final quarter of the twentieth century.

It is important that the American people be reminded now and then—and by all available means—of the sources of the food and fiber that have been available to them in greater quantities than to the peoples of other societies. It is especially important today, with the whole world newly conscious that the United States, with all its abundance, faces shortages, even in some food lines.

Agriculture that once was taken for granted is coming to the fore suddenly as a great and cherished national asset. The whole world appreciates American efficiency in the production of crops and livestock and seeks to copy it.

But this book is not a study of efficiency. It is a look at the physical aspects of our rural midlands and as such, we believe, it captures some of the spirit, some of the dedication, some of the unique character of the people who live and work in rural America.

This book cannot begin to cover all the details of so vast and varied a region as we describe. It is an overview . . . a series of paintings and sketches that accent the beauty, the variety and splendor of subjects to which an artist can address his talents as he tours Farmland, U. S. A.

Miracle of the Cornfields

Farmers for generations have said they could hear corn grow. Standing in the heart of a maturing field, one is inclined to agree with them. The sounds are there—sounds that relate to growth. Winds whisper through the tenuous tassels. Sheltered leaves flop lazily against each other. Stalks creak under the weight of swelling ears. Some lean far enough to scrape their neighbors. Plants standing at 20,000 or more to the acre elbow each other and press for space in much the manner of overcoated people in the tight rows of a football stadium. And crowded corn, as do crowded people, gives off murmurs that are distinctive if not always harmonious or separable.

Corn is a study in superlatives. It is our largest crop in terms of volume. It is our largest source of food for humans and animals. More than any other item, it is basic to the production of meat, milk and eggs. And the United States produces far more corn, and far more corn to the acre, than any other country.

In the 1830's the big corn states were Kentucky, Tennessee and Virginia. In due time, though, the center of corn production shifted northward and westward into Illinois and Iowa, and there it remains.

With the advent of hybrid corn in the early 1930's, there was a definite improvement in yields and in growth characteristics. New fast-maturing varieties could beat the frosts of September. This encouraged the expansion of the Corn Belt's boundaries, northward and westward, mainly. Corn started crowding other crops off some of the land in the rich irrigated valleys of eastern Colorado and the Nebraska Panhandle. The spread of irrigation following World War II meant further expansion of the corn zones, and much of this was in Nebraska and Kansas on land where corn had been tried and pretty well abandoned as a reliable dry-land crop. With or without irrigation, farmers pushed up their per-acre production with increasingly heavy applications of commercial fertilizer. Yesterday's bumper crop became today's commonplace, farm by farm, county by county, state by state.

The annual miracle of the cornfields is one of the few comforting offsets to the growing realization that a nation suddenly has come in sight of the end of its abundance of fossil energy. Corn is energy, and it is renewable on a colossal scale.

One of Iowa's biggest—near Odebolt.

Travelers between Omaha and Kansas City—and along other stretches of the Missouri's long course through the midlands—can take the winding river roads and find much they have missed on the main highways. There are turns and twists and rough spots, but the traffic is light, and there is time to enjoy the sheer bluffs, the timbered gullies and the lush bottomland fields. This scene is near the spot where the Kansas-Nebraska border comes to its eastern terminus at the river.

One of the popular designations of the northwestern part of Iowa is the "Great Lakes" region. One of the lakes justifying this designation is Storm Lake, pictured here from a park in the city bearing the lake's name. The time was late October, and the wind was high enough to blow up angry wrinkles and create the right mood to convince one that the lake was properly named.

Mid-week affair at an Iowa church.

Turkey production in Mid-America is pretty much where one finds it. It is not dictated certainly by conditions of soil or climate to the extent some agricultural production is. Generally, several large producers—and most turkey production is on a large scale—key their operations to a hatchery, a feed plant and a dressing plant.

Concentrations of turkeys can be found in most states of the region, with Minnesota, Texas, Iowa, Missouri, Arkansas and Colorado among the leaders. The picture here was made on a farm near Ellsworth, Ia., as turkeys were being assembled for loading into trucks for the first leg of their individual trips to the country's dinner tables, with most likely to make their final showings on Thanksgiving or Christmas.

The corn shelling picture was made at one of the Amana Colonies along the Iowa River. While Amana is noted for its distinctive home-cured hams, home-spun woolens, hand-crafted furniture and other products, its corn and its method of shelling are typically Iowan. To the southeast of Amana is Iowa City, and a few miles east of there is West Branch, where Herbert Hoover was born. Besides the modest birthplace of the 31st president, West Branch has the extensive library where Hoover's papers are housed.

Iowa State University is the center of agricultural research and teaching for a state that leads all others in several aspects of livestock and crop production. Swine on test at the Ames campus illustrate the constant search for improvement of quality in the pork which Iowa produces in greater quantities than any other state. And Iowa means restful vistas, too—right.

19

Winterset, Iowa, proclaims itself the home of the Delicious Apple and birthplace of John Wayne. It is also the place from which one may drive to any or all of seven covered bridges, the farthest only 10 miles from town. Winterset also supplies a study in the architecture of Midwestern county-seat squares. Depicted here are the buildings facing the Madison County Courthouse from the east.

The Little Brown Church in the Wildwood—Nashua, Iowa.

Fishermen on the Mississippi River where it separates northeast Iowa from Wisconsin.

There is a starkness about farm buildings when the snow lies deep on the prairies of southern Minnesota. But there is a snugness about the house and barn at the left as they stand out against the silent whiteness—a reassuring reminder of the strength of the people and the readiness of the land to flower and bear fruit as the cycle of the seasons commands. The summer picture of cows waiting their turns at the milking stanchions is witness to the fact that the land does warm up each year. It is also a reminder of the fact that Minnesota is a leading dairy state.

A field of ripe soybeans affords a study of the geometry of planting on the contour. It is a study also of the crop which in many respects has been the Midwest's sensation of the mid-twentieth century. Soybeans were around for many years before World War II, but their rise to prominence in the economy of rural America has been most dramatic since the late 40's. By the early 70's, cash sales of soybeans approached or exceeded those of corn in some of the leading corn states. This painting is of a field in southeastern Nebraska.

Illinois and Iowa are separated by the biggest of American rivers, but it's hard for travelers to see much difference in the countryside after crossing the Mississippi in either direction. The two states are at the top in production of corn, hogs and soybeans, making for a similarity in farm layouts and equipment. Illinois, having been settled ahead of Iowa, might claim more examples of pioneer architecture, but such things are hard to document. The king-sized barn, with silos to match, was spotted in northern Illinois.

Modern machinery is found most anywhere there's work to be done, and anyone who ever bucked bales onto a wagon or truck can appreciate the loading device shown in the hayfield painting.

Where the Missouri greets the Kaw

Early explorers of the Missouri took special note of a spot where the river made an abrupt turn eastward just as it was joined by the waters of another sizable stream. Some of them predicted that this would become an important center of commerce and industry.

Looking down the Missouri today from a point upstream from its meeting with the Kansas, or Kaw, one sees abundant evidence of the prediction come true. Kansas City, Mo., and Kansas City, Kan., face each other across both the Missouri and the Kaw.

This place where the rivers join did become a center of great activity and development. For many years the wagon trains went out from here to Santa Fe, Oregon and Colorado. More than 100 years ago the railroads started funneling their lines through the merging valleys. Highways came, and then the airlines. (Two airports border the river within the range of the skyline painting, and a third, Kansas City International, is just a few miles away.)

The river itself remains a route of trade. Its modern barge tows are a far cry from the johnboats of the explorers and early traders and trappers; and there is none of the romance of the days of steam and sternwheelers. But a lot of tonnage moves with the sleek and almost silent tows. When the barges are headed downstream, there's a good chance they carry grain from Iowa, Missouri, Kansas, Nebraska or Colorado. When they are headed upstream, they could be carrying fertilizer to help make grains grow.

The brick building—octagonal in shape—was once a showplace among barns—the palatial quarters of mules that drew the plows, planters and wagons on one of Missouri's largest farms. It is now the theater of Tarkio College, whose campus grew up alongside the farm. Through the door of the wooden barn in the other picture one glimpses tobacco in the curing process. Barns of this kind dot the hillsides of Missouri's tobacco belt, south of St. Joseph.

It's April, and an ancient apple tree proclaims the fact at an abandoned farmstead near Gardner, Kan. It's June, and a central Kansas housewife climbs her ladder and looks forward to the making of cherry pies. It's October, and this roadside stand in Doniphan County, Kansas, dresses up in pumpkins, apples and other vegetables and fruits.

34

The "M" in Missouri could well stand for "middle" or "mixed" among agricultural states. Annual statistics usually show Missouri in the first ten in cash value of all farm commodities. It ranks high in production of corn, hogs, and soybeans, but never has been first. It usually is among the top ten in cattle, dairy products, turkeys and grain sorghums. It produces some tobacco and cotton. It used to produce mules.

If Missouri's "M" suggests anything, though, it is mid-America. This is not strictly in a geographic sense, but in the fact that Missouri as a state is close to the national middle in a lot of ways—in its combination of prairies, woodlands, streams and Ozark uplands, in the ethnic mix of its people, in its urban-rural and industrial-agricultural balance.

And so we come to the setting of a painting that is about as typically mid-American as any in this book. It could have been in any of several states, but it is between Springfield and Joplin. The kind of storm depicted is no respecter of states, either.

37

Blue house and hollyhocks—and wash day.

Sheep through trees on a morning in October.

Early settlers in southern Missouri were quick to put the clear-flowing streams to work. They built water wheels to power grist mills such as the one shown. Some of the old mills still work, but they are more important as tourist attractions than service centers. The lake scene is on Table Rock, one of the many bodies of water created by damming the White and other Ozark rivers.

University of Arkansas buildings are the skyline beyond this vineyard on the university farm at Fayetteville. A few miles south, on the road to Van Buren and Fort Smith, one crosses the so-called Boston Mountains, a picturesque and rugged extension of the Ozark uplift, that inspired the picture at left.

43

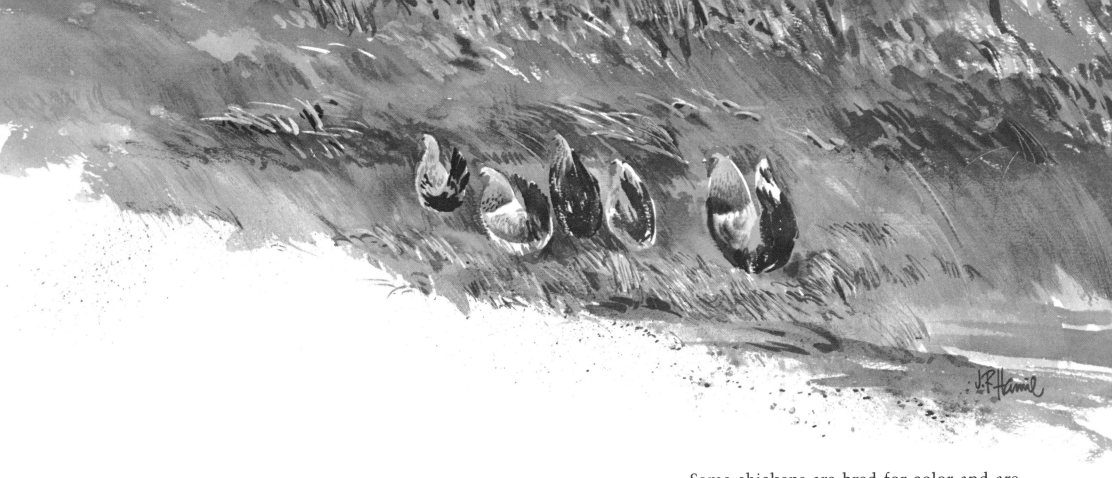

Some chickens are bred for color and are treated as pets or novelties, as are the ones pictured. But most chickens live a short and hurried life of programmed anonymity. Some are kept for the eggs they lay. Others are rushed from hatchery to dressing plant with no time to get acquainted with the world outside their crowded quarters. The broiler house in Northwest Arkansas, without a chicken in sight, speaks eloquently of the machine-like precision with which the confined birds eat and drink their way from egg to fryer. And the gate? Where it leads to and whom it serves seems less important than the design and setting.

45

About Wheat

Wheat is an annual grass and its habitat more often than not is land where grass was dominant and great herds of buffalo fed through the centuries before white men arrived.

While almost every state produces some wheat, 10 states of the Great Plains produce about 60 per cent of United States wheat in an average year. In the Dakotas and northern and eastern Montana wheat is planted in the spring and harvested in mid- and late-summer. In Texas, Oklahoma, Kansas, Nebraska, Colorado, New Mexico and Wyoming, planting is in the fall and the harvest starts in June or July. A virtue of wheat in regions of low rainfall and high summer tempera-

47

48

tures is that the crop is out of the way by the time the hottest weather arrives.

The emergence of wheat as a major export crop in the United States dates from the introduction of the so-called Turkey red wheat in Kansas by Mennonite immigrants in 1874. Agricultural and milling industry authorities credit the arrival of this new strain with establishing standards of quality on which producers and processors based plans and operations that have made wheat the dominant cash crop of Kansas and other Great Plains states.

The Alexanderwohl Mennonite Church near Goessel is one of the many reminders of the role of the Mennonites in introducing hard winter wheat to Kansas. The church was named for a community in Russia from which the Mennonites came. Wheat pouring from combine to truck illustrates the bulk of a crop that developed from the driblets of seed the Mennonite settlers brought with their luggage.

This half-mile long row of silos at Hutchinson, Kan., is a dramatic illustration of the size of the annual wheat crop as it moves from farms into national and world markets. The importance of terminal storage of this kind can be fully understood, though, only if one considers that this array of silos is duplicated in varying sizes and combinations at Wichita, Salina, Topeka, Kansas City, Omaha, Lincoln, Enid, Amarillo and other points. There are seasons, of course, when some of the space is filled with milo and other grains.

The barns at Kansas State University, Manhattan, are graceful reminders of an architectural form that is unmistakably agricultural. While newer buildings for the housing of livestock are more functional, they are far less distinctive. Old barns have something in common with old steam traction engines; they have an appeal that outlives their efficiency, and men are slow to discard them.

Old House—New Milo. There is a sturdiness in the walls of this old house on a hill near Jewell, Kan. There is elegance in the remaining embellishments. But what seems to stand out is the ability of this island of hand-cut limestone to defy the waves of change—in this case the waves of new milo that break around the steps and sills.

J.R.Hamil

Grass and Cattle

And the earth brought forth grass . . . and God saw that it was good.—Genesis 1—12.

Grass is good, and grass is basic, but it makes few headlines. It lacks the glamor of corn, wheat, cotton and other mass-produced crops. It plays second fiddle to the cattle it sustains by the millions. And only when converted to commercial hay does it make the agricultural production statistical charts.

Grasslands are measured in millions of acres. They vary widely in topography, in varieties of grasses and lushness of growth. While they sustain many sheep and horses, they figure in the national agricultural

57

picture much more importantly in their relation to cattle.

Most grasslands are in the virgin state, but there are large acreages where farmers tried to grow crops and then decided the land was better for grass. This is true in hilly country with good rainfall as well as in the high plains where attempts to grow crops were foiled by drouth and wind erosion.

The Flint Hills of Kansas are an island of grass that has remained largely untouched by the tools of cultivation. One reason, of course, is that protruding limestone (not flint) discouraged pioneers looking for land on which to grow crops. The region, extending from the Kansas River in the Topeka-Manhattan area to the southern edge of the state, is attractive not only to cattlemen, but also to countless Kansans and others who find enjoyment in driving through the curving hills when they are bright with the season's cover of bluestem (pages 56 and 57).

The sandhills of Nebraska are another distinctive grassland area. Ranchers there supplement summer grazing on the hills with winter feeding of hay cut from sub-irrigated valleys. There are vast grasslands in the Dakotas, Wyoming, Texas, Oklahoma, Colorado and New Mexico. And they all contribute to the production of beef.

The annual rodeo at Strong City, Kan., is not all riding, roping, wrestling and wrangling. There are moments when men can get together—and just talk. Especially is this true on a cold, wet day when the weather brings out jackets and forces interruptions in the schedule.

60

Limestone, in one form or another, is part of the landscape in much of Kansas. But nowhere else in the state—nowhere else in the world—does one see limestone used to support barbed wire to the extent it's used in a vast diagonal strip running from northeast to southwest on both sides of a line extending roughly from Belleville to Dodge City.

This is Post Rock Country, in the language of those who are determined to preserve its distinct heritage. The Post Rock Museum at LaCrosse includes a collection of posts, the tools with which they were quarried and shaped and much additional memorabilia of an era when the liberal expenditure of sweat and muscle was the daily routine of farm folk.

Weighing from 250 to 500 pounds, the posts were broken from ledges by a variety of methods. The most essential tool was a drill with which lines of holes were bored. Wedges were inserted in the holes and the rock was tapped with hammers until the designated section cracked loose.

The St. Fidelis "Cathedral of the Plains" at Victoria, Kan., in an area dotted with stone fence posts, was built largely from stone that came from the same quarries as the posts. St. Fidelis is in the National Register of Historic Places.

The dirt is red, so it has to be Oklahoma. The conclusion is safe for large parts of the Sooner state, but not all. It applies in this case to the northwestern part, where red soil prevails, as in the eroded bank, and grain elevators sprout from every siding.

The painting across the two preceding pages could well be titled, "Twilight on the Trail—in the Oklahoma Panhandle."

Corn may grow as high as an elephant's eye in Oklahoma, but the corn stalk is not nearly so high as an oil derrick as a symbol of the state's resources. Cattle and wheat rank with petroleum among Oklahoma's major products, but corn is pretty far down the list. The poetic license that placed corn in a popular song about Oklahoma does not alter the fact that the state ranks higher as a producer of peanuts than of corn.

Most of what is now Oklahoma was designated as Indian Territory in 1834 and barred from settlement by whites. It was the end of the Trail of Tears of the dispossessed Cherokees from southeastern states. It became the homeland of other tribes, but by the 1880's there were large tracts of land that the Indians were not using or had ceded back to the federal government. Congress yielded to growing pressure and began opening these lands to settlement. Men who jumped the gun, so to speak, in the competitive "runs" for land were called Sooners (they arrived too soon), and the nickname now applies to all Oklahomans.

American agriculture depends heavily on a vast network of underground pipes. Some carry crude oil from wells to refineries and refined fuels from these plants to final distribution points. Some carry natural gas, the only raw material—aside from water and air—required for the manufacture of nitrogen fertilizer. And there are situations in which nitrogen (in anhydrous ammonia form) moves from the manufacturing point by pipeline. Pipelines operate quietly and unseen beneath fields and pastures, across and along highways and railroads. Here and there one comes to the surface at a control point, as pictured. The night scene, at left, is of a nitrogen plant at Lawrence, Kan., where gas, air and water are converted into nitrogen fertilizer.

The McCook, Neb., home of *George W. Norris*. As a member of the House of Representatives and the United States Senate, he was a champion of the American farmer. No man did more to make rural electrification a matter of national policy.

Nebraskans call theirs the Beef State, and they refer to their state university athletic teams as Cornhuskers. Through much of their history they have worn a third sobriquet, Tree Planters. And when they look to the top of their towering state capitol at Lincoln, they see a 27-foot bronze statue of a man in the classic pose of a planter of seeds. This is officially known as The Sower, and it serves as a sort of presiding symbol over a state that has cherished and nourished its agricultural traditions.

Nebraska is among the top states in production of calves, fat cattle, hogs and corn. It ranks big in wheat, sorghum grains, sugar beets and hay. Its tree planting tradition originated in the leadership of J. Sterling Morton, an early resident who was secretary of agriculture in the cabinet of President Grover Cleveland. The former Morton home at Nebraska City is now the center of Arbor Lodge State Park. Considered the father of Arbor Day, Morton set an example in tree planting that was highly effective in what had been at the beginning an almost treeless

Willa Cather came to fame as a writer of novels based on the lives of farm folk and others in a pioneer community. Many of her characters and scenes were identified with her home town, Red Cloud, Neb. This is the family home in Red Cloud.

state. A national forest was eventually set down in the midst of Nebraska's Sandhills.

The Sower, high above the tree-lined streets of Lincoln, high above the places where Cornhuskers play, high above the fields, feedlots and pastures, has withstood drouth and depression, the wisecracks of local wags and the sarcastic comments of visiting sports writers, one of whom once likened the figure's pose to that of a Georgia crapshooter. Nebraska's agriculture, meanwhile, has grown mightily and significantly.

J.R. Hamil

A pasture, a low rock wall beneath the fence wires, a strip of pavement and a loaded cattle truck—these contribute to the picture, but a passing storm provided the distinctive touches. It brought a rainbow and laid a glassy film to be shattered into a rolling spray by the truck tires. In a simpler illustration of the way weather helps make a picture, the cattle seem more interested in the observer than in the snow on their backs.

Cattle are the true transients of American agriculture. While many grow to maturity and are fattened on the farms where they are born, many more take at least one trip by truck or train before their final journey to the packing plant. Calves from Texas sometimes winter on wheat pasture in Kansas and then move to feedlots in Nebraska or Colorado. Iowa farmers fill their lots each fall with cattle whose origins can be traced all the way to Montana. Many cattle, including breeding stock, have one or two experiences in the auction ring.

There is an appropriateness, therefore, in a picture of cattle with a loading chute. This is an essential item on any farm or ranch where cattle arrive and depart by truck. At the regional sales barns, terminal markets, larger ranches and commercial feedlots the loading equipment is more sophisticated than that shown, but the purpose is the same—to simplify the movement of animals that can change locations and owners three or more times in two years of living.

Railroads fixed the pattern of settlement of much of Mid-America and they dictated the movement of men, crops, livestock and supplies through several generations. They have given ground to autos, trucks and airplanes, but the trains still roll and the romance of the rails is far from dead. Union Pacific double-track in Nebraska, near Gibbon.

Scott's Bluff

This dramatic promontory on the plains of western Nebraska marks a spot in history. It also marks the heart of an irrigation farming area that is sometimes referred to as America's Valley of the Nile. For explorers, trappers, traders and homeseekers on the way to Oregon or California, this was a sort of outrider of the Rocky Mountains which they would encounter some distance beyond. They camped at its base, along which flows the North Platte River. When a trader named Hiram Scott died there, people started referring to Scott's Bluff, and the combination of names was adopted by a county, a city and a region. The bluff itself is a national monument.

Irrigation ditches lace the wide valley in all directions, making for lush fields of alfalfa, sugar beets, beans, corn and small grains and a steady movement of cattle from pasture to feedlot, to packing plant. The painting shows the bluff through a thin early-morning haze. Green and yellow areas in the foreground are test plots of the University of Nebraska College of Agriculture. While most irrigation in the area is from gravity-flow ditches, the sprays of a pumping system are faintly visible in the middle foreground.

78

The James River winds in a southerly direction from east-central North Dakota to join the Missouri near Yankton on the southern border of South Dakota. Shown here near its mouth, it is a lazy and placid stream whose course is so near level in places that a heavy rain starts water flowing upstream. Quiet though it is, the James is one of the longer tributaries of the Missouri. It flows past fields of wheat, flax and corn and through extensive pasture lands.

The line of the James was near the western edge of settlement in the late 19th century when large numbers of homeseekers were coming to this country from Russia. They were of German blood and had enjoyed privileges in Russia that were suddenly cut off after 100 years. If the James River country has a folk hero, it has to be Lawrence Welk. A descendant of German-Russians, he was born at Strasburg, N. D., just beyond the James basin to the west. As a young bandleader he came to prominence through broadcasts over a radio station at Yankton.

80

After more than 70 years, the Corn Palace at Mitchell, S.D., left, strikes first-time visitors much as it struck John Phillip Sousa in 1904. He had come with his band to play a series of concerts. When he saw the town, its unpaved streets and its strictly rural setting, he refused to let his muscicians get off the train. This was unbelievable to a man of Sousa's sophistication. He relaxed some when he got his $7,000 check, and he relaxed a great deal more after a warm reception by the first packed house. The Corn Palace had existed for a dozen years when Sousa first saw it. The Palace and the annual Fall Festival centering there are still going strong—taking on a new look each year—and visitors still react a lot as Sousa did. The painting here is of the 1974 version. The building is the second successor to the one Sousa saw, but the use of colored corn, other grains and grasses for decoration has been consistent down through the years.

In much of the spring wheat belt and in irrigated mountain valleys the small grain harvest usually includes windrowing. A special machine cuts the standing crop and leaves it in continuous heaps for drying and curing before the combine comes along to pick it up and thresh it. The pattern of windrows depicted here was in a spring wheat field in North Dakota.

The Old Bridger Trail once ran along the Big Horn River in this vicinity, and a stone marker a few hundred feet from this barn memorializes C. H. "Dad" Worland, who once lived in a log cabin on the site. The town of Worland, Wyo., was founded here, but was moved across the river in 1906. The barn dates from 1917.

Sugar beets in August are nearing maturity, and in a well watered field the big leaves glisten in the sun. This scene is in the valley of the Big Horn River, near Worland in north-central Wyoming. The yellow in the distance marks a field of special barley that is grown for the brewing industry. The light-weight curved pipes must be carefully "set" by hand, to siphon water from the ditch.

Snow means business and profits to the operators of ski resorts in the Colorado Rockies. To the ranchers nearby, though, it merely adds to the winter routine of feeding and protecting livestock. Machine-stacked hay acknowledges the use of modern labor-saving equipment on a place near Oak Creek. While the barn and horses in the other picture seem to have the wintry world to themselves, they are within view of a railroad, a highway and the telephone lines that extend down the Yampa Valley through Steamboat Springs, Hayden and Craig.

Across the rugged north-south center of Colorado are four distinct valleys, each adjoining the Continental Divide and each encompassing the headwaters of a river. One of these is North Park, an area of rolling pastures, lush hay meadows and clear streams that end up as the North Platte River. This view, looking west from near Walden, includes mountains north of Rabbit Ear Pass and the faint lines of a summer rainstorm.

90

The waters of the Cache La Poudre River sparkle and splash their way out of the mountains northwest of Fort Collins, Colo. The moment they reach the open plains, though, they give up their carefree ways and submit to a system of dams, ditches and reservoirs and provide life for one of the nation's most concentrated irrigation-farming areas. Horace Greeley's Union Colony dug the first ditches for tapping the Poudre, and the city that bears his name relies heavily on the agricultural economy of the area. Sugar beets are a major crop, and among the several sugar factories of the area is the one pictured, at Greeley. This is also a cattle feeding and meat packing center.

Patterns in Great Plains agriculture are an interesting study from the clouds. Green circles indicate three quarters of a 640-acre section under center-pivot pump irrigation. Dry-land strip farming of wheat land (dark strips are fallow) is indicated at bottom center of painting. The water-filled ditch extends from the South Platte River to lands near Sterling, Colo., that have been under gravity irrigation since the turn of the century. Such ditches were dug with teams and scrapers.

Texas is size and space and distance. It is
Dalhart on the high, dry plains at the northwest
and Brownsville at sea level some 800 miles to
the southeast. It is Houston, Dallas, Amarillo
and Lubbock. It is San Antonio, San Marcos,
Gonzales, Hidalgo and New Braunfels. It is
Happy, Muleshoe, Lazbuddie, Nazareth and
Dawn, with the last named being in Deaf Smith
County. It is oil, cattle, cotton, rice, horses,
sheep and goats. And it is bluebonnets in the
spring, somewhere south of Fort Worth.

Horses in a snow-laden wind on the high plains are in full agreement on one point: The best way to stand in a cold wind is with your back to it.

One of the few breaks in the flat plains of the Texas Panhandle is the course of the Canadian River. It comes out of New Mexico on the west and, after a series of sweeping curves, moves into Oklahoma. The painting is of a spot between Amarillo and Dalhart.

The lone Longhorn speaks of Texas, most any part of it. The giant oak speaks of an area near the Gulf Coast, south of Houston.

Fishermen along the Gulf Coast of Texas consider themselves a part of the food industry, along with the farmers and ranchers who operate on dry land. This shrimp boat, in drydock near Bay City, is an implement of harvest, as much as a combine is or a cotton picker. And it represents a considerable investment.

INDEX OF PAINTINGS

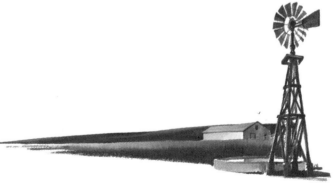